33

P9-CRE-391

13 Colonies

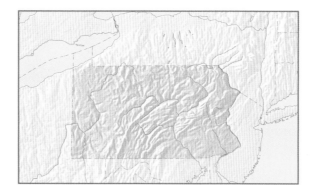

Pennsylvania

13 Colonies

PENNSYLVANIA

The History of Pennsylvania Colony, 1681–1776

ROBERTA WIENER AND JAMES R. ARNOLD

Raintree

Chicago, Illinois

For information, address the publisher:
Raintree, 100 N. LaSalle, Suite 1200, Chicago, IL 60602

Printed and bound in China

08 07 06 05 04
10 9 8 7 6 5 4 3 2 1

Library of Congress Cataloging-in-Publication Data
Wiener, Roberta, 1952-
  Pennsylvania / Roberta Wiener and James R. Arnold.
    p. cm. -- (13 colonies)
Summary: A detailed look at the formation of the colony of Pennsylvania, its government, and its overall history, plus a prologue on world events in 1681 and an epilogue on Pennsylvania today.
Includes bibliographical references and index.
  ISBN 0-7398-6886-1 (lib. bdg.) -- ISBN 1-4109-0310-9 (pbk.)
  1. Pennsylvania--History--Colonial period, ca. 1600-1775--Juvenile literature. 2. Pennsylvania--History--Revolution, 1775-1783--Juvenile literature. 3. Pennsylvania--Politics and government--1775-1783--Juvenile literature. [1. Pennsylvania--History--Colonial period, ca. 1600-1775. 2. Pennsylvania--History--Revolution, 1775-1783.] I. Arnold, James R. II. Title. III. Series: Wiener, Roberta, 1952-   13 colonies.
  F152.W56 2004
  974.8'02--DC21

                    2003011060

Title page picture: Philadelphia in 1702, twenty years after its founding, with a population close to 10,000, but still surrounded by thick woods

Opposite: The Delaware River Valley had many iron furnaces, mills, and forges. Furnaces smelted the iron ore into pig iron, mills formed the pig iron into bars, and forges shaped iron bars into finished products. By 1750, the American colonies produced one eighth of the world's pig iron.

The authors wish to thank Walter Kossmann, whose knowledge, patience, and ability to ask all the right questions have made this a better series.

Picture Acknowledgments

Authors: 38, 59 Anne S.K. Brown Military Collection, Brown University Library, Providence, RI: 58 Abby Aldrich Rockefeller Folk Art Museum, Colonial Williamsburg Foundation: Cover, 28-29 Colonial Williamsburg Foundation: 6, 11 top, 21 bottom, 26, 30, 46-47, 51 U.S. Government Printing Office: 56 Courtesy of the Historical Society of Delaware: 20, 21 top, 23 Historical Society of Pennsylvania: 35, 41 top Independence National Historical Park: 13 Library Company of Philadelphia: 52-53 Library of Congress: Title page, 7, 8, 11 bottom, 14-15, 16, 19, 22, 24, 25, 27, 31, 32-33, 40-41, 42, 44-45, 48, 49, 55 Maryland Historical Society, Baltimore, MD: 5, 43 National Archives: 36-37, 39 National Portrait Gallery, London, England: 10 Philadelphia Free Library: 34

CONTENTS

PROLOGUE: THE WORLD IN 1681

In 1681, the year the English colonists came to Pennsylvania, English people had already settled in eleven other American territories that were destined to become part of the United States.

Europe had begun to explore the wider world during the Renaissance, a 150-year period of invention and discovery. Advances in navigation and the building of better sailing ships allowed longer voyages. So began the Age of Exploration, with great seamen from Portugal, Spain, Italy, France, and England sailing into uncharted waters. Beginning in the 1400s, they reached Africa, India,

A map shows how Europeans saw the world around 1570.

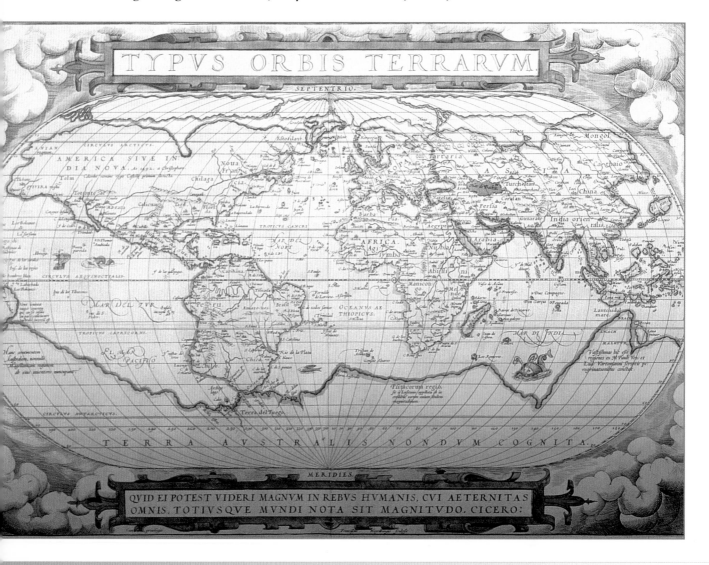

the Pacific Ocean, China, Japan, and Australia. They encountered kingdoms and civilizations that had existed for centuries.

The voyages from Europe to these distant shores went around Africa. This made the trip long and dangerous. So, European explorers began to sail westward in search of shortcuts. In 1492, the explorer Christopher Columbus landed on an island on the far side of the Atlantic Ocean and claimed it for Spain. He thought that he had actually sailed clear around the world and come to an island near India. Years of exploration by numerous sailors passed before the people of Europe realized that Columbus had been the first European of their era to set foot in a land

unknown to them. They called this land the New World, although it was not new to the people who lived there. After Columbus, Amerigo Vespucci claimed to have reached the New World. Whether he actually did or not, in 1507 a mapmaker put his name on a map, and the New World became **America**, or the Americas. Still looking for that shortcut to the riches of Asia, European explorers continued to sail to North and South America. They also began to claim large pieces of these lands for their own nations.

By the time the first English people settled in Pennsylvania, the French, mainly Roman Catholics, had founded three settlements in Canada, at Quebec, Trois Rivieres (near Quebec), and Acadia (the area around modern-day Nova Scotia). Far to the south, French Protestants had tried to start a **colony** in Florida and been driven off by the Spaniards. Several Frenchmen had explored inland North America, including the Mississippi valley, the Great Lakes, and Niagara Falls. One of them, Robert Cavalier, Sieur de La Salle, in 1669 claimed to have

France believed that the travels of French explorers in the interior of North America gave their country ownership of a vast area. LaSalle's travels expanded their claim to include the Ohio River valley and a large chunk of western Pennsylvania.

Opposite: Hernán Cortés conquered the Aztec empire and claimed Mexico for Spain. He captured the Aztec emperor, Montezuma, and took over his kingdom.

PERSECUTION: TO PUNISH PEOPLE BECAUSE OF THEIR BELIEFS, RELIGION, OR RACE

GRANT: FORMAL GIFT OF A PARCEL OF LAND

QUAKER: ORIGINALLY A TERM OF MOCKERY GIVEN TO MEMBERS OF THE SOCIETY OF FRIENDS, A CHRISTIAN GROUP FOUNDED IN ENGLAND AROUND 1650

explored the Ohio River valley, which began in western Pennsylvania.

But the Spanish were far ahead of other Europeans in the competition for land in the Americas. Before the English came to America, the Spanish had already claimed huge portions of both North and South America. They had conquered two mighty North American empires, and introduced the first domestic cattle and horses to the Americas. They founded the first two permanent cities — St. Augustine and Santa Fe — in what would become the United States. They had brought European civilization as well, including printing presses and universities. The Spanish also brought their chosen form of Christianity, Roman Catholicism, and converted hundreds of Native Americans, often by force.

Europe was no stranger to religious violence and intolerance when English people began looking for a religious haven in America. Christians had long been going to war with Muslims and **persecuting** Jews. During the 1490s, the Spanish and the Portuguese had expelled from their countries all Jews who refused to convert. European Christians had fought many wars, called Crusades, in the effort to drive Muslims from the Middle East and Europe. The Christian people of Europe also fought one another, in long and bloody wars of religion, and the English joined the fight.

For centuries in western Europe, Christianity and Roman Catholicism had been one and the same, with all Christians ruled from Rome by the Pope. But in 1517, Martin Luther, a German monk, protested some of the actions of the Roman Catholic church, and so began the Protestant Reformation. In 1534, the English King Henry VIII took advantage of the Protestant Reformation. The Pope would not **grant** him a divorce, so he formed the Church of England and declared himself its head. The Church of England, also called the Anglican church, became a Protestant church, independent of the Pope, but still Christian.

Even though under Protestant rule, many English Protestants grew dissatisfied and formed churches to practice their own versions of Christianity. Among them were the Pilgrims, the Puritans, and the **Quakers**, all of whom suffered persecution for their beliefs and eventually

Opposite: Except in Pennsylvania, Quakers were widely disliked in America. An English woman newly arrived in America met her American relatives and reported: "I met with … mortification upon hearing that my Relations were Quakers, & what was the worst of all my Aunt a Preacher. I was Sorry to hear it, for I was Exceedingly prejudiced against these People & have often wondered with what face they Could Call them Selves Christians." In spite of this initial attitude, the woman later became a Quaker.

chose to come to America. However, migration to America did not guarantee religious freedom to all. In the American colonies, Christian groups continued to persecute one another. Of the few colonial laws that extended rights to religious minorities, most explicitly stated that they referred only to Christian minorities. William Penn, founder of Pennsylvania, was truly ahead of his time. He wrote religious freedom—"freedom of Conscience," as he called it—into law for his colony right from the start. Only when the United States passed the Bill of Rights in 1791 did religious freedom and tolerance become the law of the land for all of the states.

I.
FRIENDS IN HIGH PLACES

An Englishman named George Fox founded a new Christian religion, the Friends of God, or Society of Friends, about 1650. The Friends' beliefs, behavior, and appearance set them apart from other English people and other Christians. Unlike other Christians, the Friends did not have churches, worship services, or ministers. They had meetings in simple houses, and any person could speak at any time. They believed that each person had a direct relationship with God, and so did not need a minister to act as a go-between. The Friends dressed plainly, refused to take oaths, and refused to make distinctions among social classes or use forms of respect for people in high positions. They objected to all forms of violence, including war, and refused to serve in any military group.

People mockingly called the Friends "Quakers," because their founder said they should "quake" at the word of the Lord. However, the Friends did not at first call themselves "Quakers." The Society of Friends quickly

Above: Oliver Cromwell, England's Puritan head of state from 1649 to 1658, criticized the Quakers for their "irregular and disorderly practices."

attracted many followers in England, Europe, and the American colonies. Because they stood out in a time of religious intolerance, they suffered from discrimination. English law barred Quakers from holding government offices or receiving higher education. Many were jailed for their refusal to attend Church of England services, and close to 500 died in English prisons.

The Puritans, who had split from the Church of England and founded a colony in Massachusetts, especially hated the Quakers, some of whom had come to Massachusetts in 1656. The Massachusetts colony even executed four Quakers for trying to convert people to their beliefs. In spite of widespread persecution, the Society of Friends attracted new members in most of England's American colonies.

William Penn, the well-educated son of a wealthy and prominent English family, became a Quaker at the age of 22. English authorities jailed him four times for trying to convert others to his beliefs. He could have avoided prison because his father, Admiral Sir William Penn, was a good friend of King Charles II. By serving his jail sentences, Penn won the trust of other Quakers and became one of their leaders.

Admiral Penn, William's father, had loaned money to King Charles II and helped him to regain the throne of England in 1660. King Charles II's brother James, the future king of England, was the Duke of York. When the royal family returned to England, Admiral Penn and the Duke of York ran England's navy department together. The long family friendship played a key role in the founding of Pennsylvania. The king could not repay the money he owed Admiral Penn before the admiral's death in 1670. So in 1681, when William Penn became interested in starting a colony in America, the king granted him a large piece of land, about 45,000 square miles, and a charter to colonize it. Penn and a number of other Quakers already shared ownership of the colony of New Jersey, but Penn wanted more land and complete control of its government.

The charter of 1681 also gave the new colony its name, Pennsylvania—Penn in honor of the late Admiral Penn, and sylvania, meaning woods. As the **proprietor**, William Penn also received a great deal of authority over

PROPRIETOR: PRIVATE OWNER

Pennsylvania's government. Penn called the colony his "Holy Experiment." He planned to govern the colony according to Quaker beliefs, especially pacifism and religious tolerance.

Penn also hoped to make money from his colony by selling or leasing land, and trading for furs with the Native Americans. He immediately set to work to publicize the colony, writing and publishing a pamphlet called, "Some

William Penn was born in 1644 and died in 1718. He visited his colony only twice: from 1682 to 1684 and from 1699 to 1701. Penn received a good education, but was expelled from Oxford for refusing to attend Anglican church. He had heard a Quaker speaker while he was still in his early teens, and thereafter been attracted to the Society of Friends.

Account of the Province of Pennsilvania." He took great care to publish only the facts, rather than to tempt settlers by making the land sound better than it was. Penn had not yet visited the land, but interviewed people who had seen it so he could give a truthful account. He warned potential colonists that "they must look for a Winter before a Summer comes; and they must be willing to be two or three years without some of the conveniences they enjoy at home."

William Penn met with King Charles II, who granted him his vast colony. In 1681, Penn gratefully wrote, "by the good providence of God a Country in America is fallen to my lot. ..."

2.
PENN'S WOODS IN 1681

Pennsylvania is a land of mountains and rivers. The Allegheny Mountains extend across the colony from southwest to northeast. A small triangle of the Piedmont and Coastal Plain forms the southeastern section of Pennsylvania. The soils of this section, which surrounds Philadelphia, are fertile and excellent for farming.

The Delaware River serves as the boundary with New Jersey. This river provides Pennsylvania's connection with the Atlantic Ocean. The Lehigh and Schuylkill Rivers flow into the Delaware River. In central Pennsylvania, the wide and shallow Susquehanna is the most important river. In the west, the Allegheny and Monongahela Rivers join at present-day Pittsburgh to form the mighty Ohio River.

North and west of the Piedmont are a series of valleys, each separated by a ridge of mountains. These wide, long valleys provided routes leading west for the colony's settlers. The rugged Appalachian Plateau makes up the western half

The Lehigh River in colonial times was shaded by thick woods, as was much of the Pennsylvania landscape. Oak, poplar, beech, ash, gum, hickory, sassafras, walnut, chestnut, and pine trees all grew in the colony.

of Pennsylvania. It consists of numerous small valleys and broken ridge lines. The highest mountain in Pennsylvania, Mt. Davis, stands 3,213 feet (980 meters) tall in the north.

Pennsylvania has trees typical of both northern and southern forests. When the first colonists came to Pennsylvania, forests covered almost the entire colony. William Penn wrote in 1681, "For timber and other wood there is a variety for the use of man." Wildlife was abundant including black bear, deer, and fur-bearing mammals suitable for trapping, with numerous fish in the streams and rivers. Penn wrote, "For Fowl, Fish, and Wild-Deer, they are reported to be plentiful in those Parts."

Pennsylvania's climate is marked by wide temperature variations. Temperatures in southeastern Pennsylvania are slightly higher, and the climate milder. All of Pennsylvania receives enough rainfall for growing crops. Pennsylvania is warmer than New England, but cooler than Maryland and Virginia, combining a long growing season with comparative freedom from mosquito-borne diseases such as malaria.

Before the first Europeans settled Pennsylvania, about 12,000 Native Americans belonging to one of four major groups lived or hunted there: Iroquois, Leni-Lenape (called Delawares by the Europeans), Susquehannock, and

Black bears have been greatly reduced in number since colonial times, but a few can still be seen in remote, unpopulated areas of Pennsylvania.

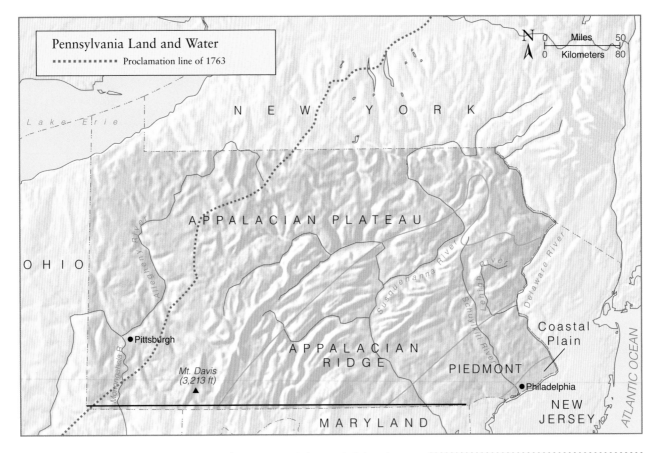

Pennsylvania Land and Water

········· Proclamation line of 1763

N

0   Miles   50
0   Kilometers   80

N E W   Y O R K

A P P A L A C I A N   P L A T E A U

O H I O

Allegheny River

Susquehanna River

Lehigh River

Schuylkill River

Delaware River

Coastal
Plain

●Pittsburgh

Monongahela R.

Mt. Davis
(3,213 ft)
▲

A P P A L A C I A N
R I D G E

P I E D M O N T

●Philadelphia

ATLANTIC OCEAN

N E W
J E R S E Y

M A R Y L A N D

Shawnee. Earlier European settlements in the neighboring colonies—New York, New Jersey, Delaware, and Maryland—had already forced many of these Native Americans to migrate to Pennsylvania. The Europeans carried diseases such as measles and **smallpox**. The native peoples had never been exposed to these diseases and had no natural resistance to them. They died by the thousands in at least seven **epidemic**s that occurred in the 50-year period after the first Europeans, the Dutch, arrived in the Native Americans' homelands.

In early times, Iroquois hunters and warriors moved through Pennsylvania. Later, they established permanent homes along the border with New York. Because of their **alliance** with other Native Americans, known as the **Iroquois Confederacy**, they were an important force in the colony. They gained influence over the Delawares and the Susquehannocks as they each sought refuge in Pennsylvania.

The Delawares lived along the Delaware River, in parts of Pennsylvania, New Jersey, and New York. Dutch,

EPIDEMIC: WIDESPREAD OUTBREAK OF CONTAGIOUS DISEASE; FOR EXAMPLE, IN 1639, A SMALLPOX EPIDEMIC KILLED HALF OF ALL HURON INDIANS

ALLIANCE: AGREEMENT TO COOPERATE, OR TO FIGHT ON THE SAME SIDE IN A WAR

Opposite: A Susquehannock village, is portrayed by a European artist of the time. The palm trees were imaginary, but the stockade and houses are more realistic.

SMALLPOX: HIGHLY CONTAGIOUS AND WIDE-SPREAD DISEASE THAT CAUSED PAINFUL SKIN ERUPTIONS, SCARRING, AND OFTEN DEATH, UNTIL IT WAS NEARLY WIPED OUT BY VACCINATION IN THE 20TH CENTURY. THE DISEASE DID NOT OCCUR AMONG NATIVE AMERICANS UNTIL THEY CAUGHT IT FROM THE FIRST EUROPEANS.

Swedish, and English colonization of their land pushed the Delawares into Pennsylvania, where yet another English colony caught up with them in 1681.

The Susquehannocks lived to the north and west of the Delawares, along the Susquehanna River in New York, Pennsylvania, and Maryland. Their ancestors had been living in stockaded towns since the 1300s. Their largest town, built around 1645 in present-day Lancaster County, covered about 12 acres and held close to three thousand people. The Susquehannocks took land from several groups of Delawares during the 1630s.

The Susquehannocks had only stone tools before they met and traded with Europeans. European trade brought them metal tools and cooking pots, and guns and ammunition. Most Susquehannock townspeople depended on farming and trade for their survival, while others still lived by hunting and fishing.

During the 1640s the Susquehannocks were at war with both the Iroquois to the north and the English settlers of Maryland to the south. Unable to continue fighting a war on two fronts, the Susquehannocks made peace with

Maryland and gave up much of their Maryland territory in 1652. The Iroquois finally conquered the last of the Susquehannocks in 1676. Their population had been so reduced by decades of almost constant warfare and repeated epidemics that they couldn'y fight any longer.

The Iroquois Confederacy claimed the Susquehannocks' former lands in southern Pennsylvania, and forced the few survivors to move to New York. The Iroquois then ordered displaced Delawares to settle on the Susquehannocks' former Pennsylvania land.

Groups of Shawnees also lived along the Ohio River, the Susquehanna River, and near the present-day town of Easton, on the Delaware River. Another Native American tribe of Pennsylvania was the Erie, who lived in the northwestern corner along the shores of Lake Erie. However, the Eries had dispersed and left the area by the time William Penn colonized Pennsylvania. In addition, various groups of Native Americans moved through the colony while hunting for wild game, and set up temporary homes as they traveled north and south.

The first European colonists, Swedes and Finns, came to Penn's Woods by way of New Sweden, which was centered near present-day Wilmington, Delaware. New Sweden's governor in 1643 established the capital just up the Delaware River on Tinicum Island, which today lies in Pennsylvania. Dutch traders from New Netherland, which once existed in present-day New York, then built trading posts on the Pennsylvania side of the Delaware River.

Governor Johan Printz arrived at Fort Christina (present-day Wilmington, Delaware) to govern New Sweden in 1643, and ordered a new capital to be built on nearby land that would later be part of Pennsylvania.

ARRIVAL OF GOV. PRINTZ AT FORT CHRISTINA

3.
ARRIVALS AND DEPARTURES

William Penn sent his cousin William Markham to Pennsylvania to claim the land, declare his authority over the several hundred settlers already living there, and mark the boundaries of the future city of Philadelphia, "the City of Brotherly Love." Markham arrived in June 1681. The first shipload of colonists sailed from England in October 1681. When Penn himself arrived in 1682, the colony already had 4,000 settlers from England, Scotland, and Wales, and Philadelphia had 80 houses. Pennsylvania's first settlers benefited from the existence of the neighboring colonies, from which they could obtain food and supplies. Many family groups came on the first ships, so that Pennsylvania's European population quickly grew through the birth of children, as well as through immigration.

One of Penn's first official acts as governor was to call a meeting of the council and assembly to pass the Great Law, which guaranteed freedom of religion in Pennsylvania. The December 4, 1682, meeting of the assembly in the town of

When William Penn visited his colony, he stayed at his house in Philadelphia.

A German minister who came to Pennsylvania in 1750 described a voyage as miserable as any endured by colonists a hundred years earlier. Trans-Atlantic voyages still lasted up to three months. He complained of "old and sharply salted food and meat," and "very bad and foul water … very black, thick and full of worms....Add to this want of provisions, hunger, thirst, frost, heat, dampness … together with other trouble, as the lice abound so frightfully, especially on sick people, that they can be scraped off the body. The misery reaches the climax when a gale rages for 2 or 3 nights and days, so that every one believes that the ship will go to the bottom with all human beings on board."

SURPLUS: EXTRA

EXPORT: TO SEND
MERCHANDISE OUT OF THE
COUNTRY FOR SALE

Chester marked the first representative government for the colony. Voters in the three counties of Chester, Philadelphia, and Bucks each elected representatives to the assembly, while council members were appointed. Membership in the council or assembly was restricted to "freemen" who owned at least 50 acres of land. Landowners had to pay a small rent of only pennies per 100 acres. Every male indentured servant was to receive 50 acres on completion of his term of servitude.

The assembly also passed laws providing support for poor people, fining people for fighting, and banning cruel sports. Pennsylvania's guarantee of freedom of religion meant that the colony did not have an established, government-sponsored church, so colonists did not have to pay taxes to support the church.

Penn recruited a group of Quaker investors to finance the settlement of Pennsylvania. During 1682 and 1683, the investors paid the costs of sending more than 50 shiploads of colonists across the Atlantic Ocean. The land around Philadelphia was so fertile that the colony harvested enough **surplus** food to **export** during its first year of existence.

An almshouse, or house for the poor, in Philadelphia. Even poor colonists had the opportunity to escape poverty. One could acquire land by starting out as a tenant farmer, or learn a skilled trade by starting out as an apprentice. But poverty still trapped some people, especially in the cities. One writer reported reported that Quakers "dispense their charity to the poor and needy, without any regard to particular sect or party."

The Indentured Servant

Indentured servants who came to Pennsylvania often went to work for businesses. A servant with blacksmithing skills, for example, might be indentured to a blacksmith who needed help. William Penn said that if people left Europe to come to a colony such as his, "their Industry there is worth more than if they stayed at home …"

A successful farm or business in the colonies required a lot of work to make it succeed. Indentured servitude provided a farmer or businessman with workers, and gave poor people a way to move to the colonies. Indentured servitude was based on a deal between two people: A colonist paid the cost of a person's voyage across the Atlantic Ocean in exchange for four to seven years of work.

The New England colonies had a high population and a small land area, compared to the other colonies. So New England farmers did not often need to purchase servants to help with farm work. Instead, they apprenticed their sons to tradesmen in towns so they could learn skilled trades. The plantation owners of the southern colonies relied on slaves to work the land. The middle colonies, including Pennsylvania, had the most use for indentured servants, especially to help with farm work. Businessmen in the colonies also contracted indentured servants to work in skilled trades and manufacturing.

Businessmen recruited servants in Europe and then sold their indentures, or contracts, to settlers when they arrived in the colonies. One poor Englishman described his decision to become an indentured servant. He was approached by a stranger who turned out to be a "man broker," one who gets paid a small amount by a ship's captain to recruit people willing to become indentured servants. The broker bought the potential servant a beer and told him about America. The future servant decided that he "had rather leave a place where I have no prospect of advancing myself, than to continue here where I have no Friends to relieve me." He signed for five years of service in exchange for passage on a voyage to Philadelphia in 1729. The broker escorted him to an office to sign an indenture agreement, then took him out to the ship.

Between 1700 and 1775, almost half of all indentured servants went to Pennsylvania, about 50,000 from Great Britain and Ireland, and close to 20,000 from Germany. Their indenture contracts also gave the German servants arriving in Philadelphia two weeks to find successful friends or family members to pay to redeem them from servitude. Therefore, the German servants were called "redemptioners." German immigrants often signed indentures that required their whole family to be kept together. German farmers in Pennsylvania preferred to have German family groups work for them.

During their years of servitude, servants received only food, clothing, and shelter. When they earned their freedom, they were supposed to receive from their masters food, clothing, and tools with which to make a fresh start. In addition, freed male servants received 50 acres of land. Former servants often became successful enough to buy servants of their own.

Religious Refugees

William Penn intended his "Holy Experiment" to shelter all manner of religious people who fled persecution in their native countries. In addition to Quakers from England, Penn invited German Quakers and Mennonites to purchase land and settle in Pennsylvania.

The Mennonite church, named after a Dutch priest, Menno Simons, formed in Switzerland in 1525. The Mennonites, and similar Protestant groups, lived apart from society in Switzerland, Germany, and other countries of Europe. They were persecuted by violence and by laws that denied them the rights of other citizens. Mennonites came to America to escape persecution and to be permitted to worship as they pleased.

During the 1690s, A Swiss Mennonite left the church to found the Amish church, which was more strict in its practices. Both Mennonite and Amish people sought personal religious experience in their worship, lived simply in farming communities, and were against war. Amish people settled alongside the Mennonites in Lancaster County during the early 1700s.

Another European church, the Moravian church, began in the 1400s as a Christian religious movement in a part of eastern Europe called Moravia. A very small group of people kept the religion going in secret in spite of centuries of persecution by Catholics. A few families fled from Moravia to Saxony, a part of present-day Germany, and settled on the land of a sympathetic Lutheran, Count Nikolaus Ludwig von Zinzendorf, in 1722.

Moravians sail up the Delaware River to settle in Pennsylvania.

People from the area who belonged to other religious groups flocked to join the Moravians. The Moravians attended the Lutheran church in Germany, but also held a lot of extra services outside the church. When Zinzendorf realized how old the Moravian religion was, he helped the Moravians to revive their old traditions.

After 1727 the Moravians formed church-run, Moravians-only communities with daily worship services and boarding schools. Single women and men lived in separate dormitories. The Moravians began a worldwide missionary movement to spread their religion. The first Moravians came to America to work among the slaves of the West Indies in 1732. From there they migrated to Georgia to convert the Indians. Failing in Georgia, they came to Pennsylvania in 1740, where they founded the villages of Bethlehem and Nazareth. The Moravians planned to get other German church groups in Pennsylvania to unite with their church. Their plan of union did not succeed, but the Moravian church stayed in Pennsylvania and survived.

Pennsylvania's religious freedom also attracted Presbyterians from Scotland. Several Presbyterian congregations in Philadelphia, with members from England, Scotland, Wales, and Ireland, were organized in 1706. So many Scottish people immigrated to Pennsylvania during the 1700s that the majority of Pennsylvania's Christians were Presbyterians by the time of the Revolution. The Scotch-Irish who moved to the western frontier were also Presbyterians, but many lived too far from one another to organize congregations. A minister traveling to western Pennsylvania wrote in 1772, "I preached two sermons to a serious & attentive audience. Some of the settlers here had not heard a sermon for 14 years."

Bethlehem, founded by the Moravian church in 1740, was an entirely Moravian town for about 100 years.

Many English people and colonists enjoyed the "sport" of cockfighting, in which specially bred roosters fought to the death while spectators bet on which would win. Pennsylvania's Quaker government outlawed cruel sports, which also included tormenting large animals like bears and wildcats.

IMMIGRANT: PERSON WHO ENTERS A NEW COUNTRY TO SETTLE THERE PERMANENTLY

In 1683 the first German **immigrants** to America, a group of Quakers and **Mennonites**, bought 25,000 acres from Penn near Philadelphia. This became the town of Germantown, the first of many German settlements in Pennsylvania. Greater numbers of Germans soon joined these early immigrants, after a German prince converted to Catholicism and began persecuting other Christians. Years of warfare in the German provinces also drove many Germans to America.

WILLIAM PENN AND THE NATIVE AMERICANS

Penn insisted that his colonists treat Native Americans fairly. He instructed his deputies that native peoples must receive equal treatment under the law. Any disputes between Native Americans and European settlers were supposed to be heard by a panel of six European and six Native Americans. Penn also ordered that treaties be made with the Native Americans for land purchases. The colonial government paid the Native Americans 1,200 pounds (English money) for the first land it purchased along the western side of the Delaware River. By 1682 the population of the Delawares had been sharply reduced by disease. The small remaining population sold their land without protest. However, so vaguely did the treaties state the boundaries of the purchased land that arguments later broke out between the Native Americans and William Penn's descendants.

William Penn offered refuge in his colony to Native Americans displaced from neighboring colonies such as Maryland. He allowed them to settle along the lower Susquehanna River, replacing the defeated Susquehannocks. The area around a settlement called Conestoga (south of present-day Lancaster) especially became home to numerous displaced Native Americans: Delawares, Shawnees, Nanticokes, and Conoys all settled there as living in their homelands grew more difficult. The Shawnees and Delawares formed a lasting alliance during their years living side by side in Conestoga.

PENNSYLVANIA, DELAWARE, AND MARYLAND

William Penn was concerned because his colony did not have direct access to the sea. So the Duke of York (later King James II), who had been a good friend of William Penn's

By 1683 Pennsylvania's early colonists were already exporting lumber. An Englishman, impressed by his Swedish neighbors' skill with the axe, reported, "… they will build, and hardly use any other tool but an ax; They will cut down a tree, and cut him off when down, sooner than two men can saw him, and rend him into planks or what they please; only with the ax and wooden wedges …"

William Penn first met with the Delaware to make a treaty in 1682. Penn respected the Native Americans and admired their simple way of life, writing "They care for little because they want but little, and the reason is, a little contents them … if they are ignorant of our pleasures, they are also free from our pains. They are not disquieted with Bills of Lading and Exchange, nor perplexed with Chancery-Suits and Exchequer-Reckonings." The Delawares repaid Penn's good treatment with loyalty. An observer reported in 1683, "I have heard one [Delaware] say 'Swede no good, Dutch man no good, but Englishman good'."

father, gave Penn the three counties of Delaware in 1682. Penn instructed the three lower counties to elect delegates to the assembly of Pennsylvania. Lord Baltimore of Maryland also claimed ownership of Delaware. The colony of Maryland, which had existed since 1634, shared a long border with Pennsylvania. Over the years mapmakers friendly with Maryland's proprietors had cleverly moved the northern border of Maryland a bit farther north when they drew a new map. As soon as William Penn became proprietor of Pennsylvania, Lord Baltimore, proprietor of Maryland, challenged the location of their shared border, as well as Penn's claim to the Delaware counties.

Penn sailed to England in 1684 to defend his land from Maryland's claims. He encountered and overcame serious difficulties in England. He was accused of treason for not supporting the new king and queen, William and Mary, who had driven his friend James II from the throne. The

King James II ruled for barely three years, from 1685 to 1688. He was a Catholic, which many English people found objectionable, and he tried to bypass Parliament in making laws. Discontented Protestants in England wrote to James' Protestant nephew—who was also his son-in-law—William of Orange. William lived in the Netherlands with his wife Mary, daughter of James II, but also a Protestant. William landed in England with an army, and James fled to France, leaving the throne to King William III and Queen Mary II. Mary died in 1694, but William ruled England from 1689 to 1702 (below).

LEGISLATURE: GROUP OF
REPRESENTATIVES
ELECTED TO MAKE LAWS

PACIFIST: PERSON AGAINST
WAR AND VIOLENCE; THE
BELIEFS OF SUCH A PERSON

William Penn (standing with hat on) grew disappointed with the way his fellow Quakers argued with one another and with him about how to govern Pennsylvania.

Crown took over Pennsylvania as a royal colony from 1692 to 1694, in part because its Quaker-controlled **legislature** refused to vote funding for the military while England was at war. England placed a military governor over the colony, but he too failed to gain Quaker support for the war. Through careful negotiations with the king and government officials, Penn eventually regained control of his colony.

Penn finally returned to America in 1699. On his return, he found that the representatives of the Pennsylvania and Delaware counties could not cooperate. The Pennsylvanians resented having to share power with the Delaware counties, and the Delaware representatives resented the **pacifist** beliefs of the Pennsylvania Quakers. Fearing that he would lose the Delaware counties entirely, in 1702 William Penn permitted their delegates to meet separately from those of Pennsylvania. Their laws still had to be approved by Pennsylvania's governor, and the

governor also remained in charge of appointing Delaware's judges and other legal officials.

The Penn family and the Lords Baltimore, meanwhile, continued their dispute over Delaware for almost 75 years. They became involved in a lawsuit, which the British courts finally settled in the Penns' favor in 1750.

The descendants of William Penn and Lord Baltimore decided to hire the English surveyors Charles Mason and Jeremiah Dixon to survey Maryland's border with Pennsylvania and Delaware. The two men began work in 1763 and finished in 1767. Their survey created the Mason-Dixon Line, which consists of Maryland's northern border with Pennsylvania and its eastern border with Delaware. This line separating the north from the south has remained

important to Americans, as a symbol of the division between the North and the South during the Civil War.

WILLIAM PENN'S LAST JOURNEY

In spite of William Penn's belief that Quakers following their religious principles could live in harmony, Pennsylvania's government and population began to divide itself into rival factions. Free from persecution by non-Quakers, Pennsylvania's Quakers began to argue among themselves. Rich Quakers disagreed with the less wealthy Quakers over which part of the government should have the most authority. The wealthy people wanted the appointed council to have most of the power to make laws. The less wealthy wanted the elected

Philadelphia in 1702, twenty years after its founding, had a population close to 10,000, but was still surrounded by thick woods.

A Quaker woman wearing the simple clothing of her faith. Single women could conduct business, but a married woman had to have her husband's cooperation to do so. In 1718 Pennsylvania passed a law allowing a married woman to conduct business if her husband was absent for a long time. If and when the husband returned, the wife again lost the right to conduct business.

The Chester, Pennsylvania, Quaker meeting house, built in 1693. Quakers in America received constant criticism from other colonists and the authorities in London for their refusal to participate in or financially support military defense. Yet some of their ideals became an important part of American life, especially their belief in equality. The Quakers' objection to slavery and their belief in equal treatment for all found later expression in the abolition of slavery and the civil rights movement. Quakers' simplicity of attitude toward people of all economic classes also became a characteristic of the general American population.

assembly to have the most power. The council and the assembly fought so fiercely over their authority that the government almost came to a standstill. The poorer Quakers resented the richer Quakers for having the first chance to buy the best land in the colony. The poorer Quakers also wanted to see their religion become more strict.

So fierce was the fighting between the two houses of the legislature that Penn changed the colony's form of government in 1701, giving the legislature only one house, the elected assembly. This one-house legislature was unique among the American colonies. However, even the one-house legislature fought with the governor about the Penn family's control over all land purchases.

William Penn returned to England in 1701, once again to defend his claim to his colony. **Parliament** had moved to place all proprietary colonies under the control of the Crown. Penn's many friends in the English government again helped him to hold onto Pennsylvania. However, Penn had lost money on the colony and decided to sell his rights to it. Instead he fell ill and became too disabled to conduct business. The sale never took place, and Penn's second wife, Hannah, managed the colony's affairs. William Penn died in 1718, and his three sons by Hannah Penn inherited the proprietorship of Pennsylvania upon her death eight years later. Of the three, Thomas Penn played the greatest role in the colony. He came to Pennsylvania in 1732, planning to sell much of the land to settlers and make his family wealthy once again.

4.
A GROWING COLONY

The new proprietor, Thomas Penn, had no trouble attracting colonists to buy land in Pennsylvania. Even a family of modest means could become owner of a farm of more than 100 acres, while in Europe one could hope only to rent a much smaller plot. The soil was fertile, producing up to three times as much wheat as soil in Europe. Pennsylvania colonists did not have to pay to support an established church, nor did they face being drafted into military service.

Close to 100,000 Germans of various Protestant religious groups came to Pennsylvania, eventually making up a third of the colony's population. The earliest German immigrants had settled outside of Philadelphia, while later ones took up land in Lancaster County, to the west. Alarmed by their high numbers, Pennsylvania's English authorities began requiring all immigrants to take loyalty

A religious settlement in Lancaster County, drew many religious German immigrants.

Left: A colonial grist mill. Wheat flour was highly valued because it was finer than corn meal and made better bread. Pennsylvania's flour earned a good reputation because it was inspected. A mill that ground wheat into flour was called a grist mill.

oaths, and considered requiring all public officials to speak English. Many German colonists were dedicated, skilled, and hard-working farmers who improved their land and created prosperous farms. German farmers introduced the idea of keeping their livestock in barns during the winter, which kept the animals warmer so they required less feed. They also collected the manure from the barns and used it to fertilize their fields.

Between 1717 and 1760, about 30,000 **Scotch-Irish** immigrants came to Pennsylvania. They were not Irish, but actually Scottish people who had lived in Ulster, Northern Ireland. Driven from Ireland by poverty, they wanted a chance to own land. Because they were mostly Presbyterians, a Protestant sect, Pennsylvania's combination of religious tolerance and abundant territory attracted them. Some settled the western **frontier** areas of Pennsylvania, while others moved into the Shenandoah Valley of Virginia. The Scotch-Irish were not as skilled at farming as the Germans, nor did they care about the rights of Native Americans as did the Quakers. When their farms grew less productive as the soil grew less fertile, they moved on and took whatever land they could find, regardless of the Native Americans' claim to it.

PENN'S DESCENDANTS AND THE NATIVE AMERICANS

Thomas Penn's main challenge was to find enough land for all the new colonists. To do so, he had to purchase it from the Native Americans, as his father had wished.

Below: The house of James Logan, William Penn's ambitious secretary

A typically sturdy and well-built Pennsylvania German house. A Pennsylvania colonist wrote to his relatives in England, "The winter is sharp and the cattle are hard to keep. The people that come must work and know country affairs ...." Nobody knew country affairs like the Pennsylvania German colonists.

Pennsylvania German Inventions

During the 1700s German immigrants to Pennsylvania applied their farming skills and their craftsmanship to solving the challenges of succeeding in a new land. The German settlers cooperated in putting up buildings, gathering for sociable "barn-raisings." Neighbors helped new settlers put up houses and barns in a matter of days. The Pennsylvania Germans built large and sturdy barns of stone and wood. The large barns sheltered livestock during the winter. Animals wintering in barns stayed warmer than animals that were kept outside, so they needed less feed to keep their weight up.

Rather than use the small carts that colonists typically used to haul their produce to market, Pennsylvania German farmers developed the Conestoga wagon, named after Conestoga Creek, near their settlements in Lancaster County. The huge wagon had a bed that angled up at each end, so that the load would not roll off while the wagon jostled along rough roads. The Pennsylvania Germans then bred huge horses to pull the wagons. Such large horses, almost twice as heavy as typical riding horses, are called draft horses, because they were bred to draw, or drag, heavy loads. The Conestoga wagon was the forerunner to the covered wagons used by American pioneers moving west during the 1800s.

The Pennsylvania long rifle is another product of Pennsylvania German craftsmen. It later became known as the "Kentucky rifle" because so many settlers took one to Kentucky. Each handcrafted rifle was simply made and easy to repair, lightweight and easy to carry, and accurate for its time. It was designed to use smaller bullets, allowing settlers, who had to make their own bullets, to save money on lead.

Frontier dwellers often kept their long rifles over their cabin doors, so they could grab a weapon on the way out.

Conestoga wagon

Draft horses such as these can each weigh twice as much as the typical horse. They can pull heavy loads, and their extra large and wide hooves act almost like snowshoes and do not easily sink into mud or snow.

William Penn's sons were not devout Quakers. They shared neither their father's religious devotion nor his desire to protect the Native Americans' land rights. Helped by James Logan, his late father's secretary, Thomas Penn plotted the infamous Walking Purchase.

European settlement during the 1700s had pushed the Delawares off their land. They left their lands in Delaware, New Jersey, and eastern Pennsylvania, moving westward. Smallpox and measles epidemics continued to reduce their numbers. The Delawares tried to build alliances with the Iroquois and other tribes, and to protect their land by selling it off a little at a time.

The Walking Purchase was designed to drive the

Delawares from the Lehigh Valley, the last of their land in eastern Pennsylvania. Thomas Penn claimed that an old, unregistered deed from 1686 gave the English the right to all the land that a man could walk in a day and a half. He pressured the Delaware leaders to approve and sign the deed again in 1736. On September 18, 1737, Penn's agents hired men to run in relays on cleared roads, when they should have had one man walk. The Native American witnesses could not keep up with the changing cast of runners, who covered 55 miles. They were forced to give up a huge tract of land. The Native Americans' descendants remained bitter over the swindle for centuries.

Some Delawares stayed and tried to fight the Walking

Above: German missionaries translated Christian hymns into the language of the Delaware and printed a hymn book in 1763. It is believed to be the only one of its kind. A German-language press began operating in Pennsylvania in 1738.

Left: Log cabins, first built by Swedish settlers, became popular among settlers in Pennsylvania. A group of cooperating neighbors could build one in a few days.

Purchase, but the Iroquois ordered them to leave in 1742. The Iroquois received generous gifts from Pennsylvania officials in exchange for their cooperation in controlling the Delawares and making them move on. Since 1701, the Iroquois had forged a strong and lasting alliance with the English. For many years, about 10,000 Iroquois controlled trade, migration, and the lives of some 20,000 Delawares and other Native Americans whom the Iroquois had resettled on the land of the defeated Susquehannocks.

Most of the Delawares uprooted by the Walking Purchase moved to the Susquehanna Valley, joining members of about eight different displaced Native American groups, often sharing the same villages.

The most important of these villages, Conestoga, held hundreds of Native Americans and became the site for trade and negotiation with colonists. The Penn family had held the deed to the land around Conestoga from 1700, but let the Native Americans stay as long as no Europeans wanted the land. But by the 1720s, growing numbers of colonists began pushing the Native Americans out of Conestoga. Most of the Native Americans moved yet again, to the northern and western parts of Pennsylvania.

An early settler's cabin, near present-day Harrisburg, the capital of modern Pennsylvania. During most of the colonial period, the area around Harrisburg remained Native American country.

The Delaware River valley had many iron furnaces, mills, and forges. Furnaces smelted the iron ore into pig iron, mills formed the pig iron into bars, and forges shaped iron bars into finished products. By 1750 the American colonies produced one eighth of the world's pig iron.

GREAT BRITAIN: NATION FORMED BY ENGLAND, WALES, SCOTLAND, AND NORTHERN IRELAND; "GREAT BRITAIN" CAME INTO USE WHEN ENGLAND AND SCOTLAND FORMALLY UNIFIED IN 1707

COMMERCE AND INDUSTRY

As the growing population of Pennsylvania began producing manufactured goods, British manufacturers feared the competition from cheaper colonial goods. They demanded laws to stop the colonies from making competing products. At the same time, they wanted the cheaper raw materials that the colonies offered, such as lumber and **pig iron**. A series of British laws, called navigation laws, aimed to control the shipping of materials and goods by the colonies so that **Great Britain** would get the greatest benefit from the colonies' production. America was to provide the raw materials, and Britain the finished products. The main advantage the navigation laws gave to the colonists was that the British navy protected colonial trading ships from pirates and foreign enemies. Most of Pennsylvania's trade passed through the busy port of Philadelphia. The city's **merchants** took a sharp interest in the navigation laws because these laws controlled their ability to make money.

The streets of Philadelphia were laid out in rectangular blocks. Houses were built of brick to prevent the spread of both disease and fire. Many other towns suffered devastating fires because they had wooden buildings standing close together. Philadelphia rapidly became the largest city in the colonies.

The navigation laws resulted in the colonies importing much more than they exported. Finished goods such as fine dishes, clothing, or furniture were much desired by any colonists who could afford them. Colonial merchants, even Quakers known for their honesty, disobeyed navigation laws because they believed the laws were unfair. American ships illegally traded directly with the Spanish, French, and Dutch, smuggling goods to and from ports in Europe and the West Indies. The British did not have enough ships or officers to enforce laws and inspect cargos. Since smuggling was and is an illegal activity, nobody kept written records of

The work of Philadelphia's cabinet and furniture makers was in demand throughout the colonies. This photo is of a reconstruction of a colonial furniture maker's workshop.

The colonies were forbidden to make their own coins, so they used whatever coins they could obtain from other countries, such as this French coin. The colonies started producing paper money because they couldn't obtain enough coins. Pennsylvania began issuing paper currency in 1723. On the frontier, people bartered, or traded, for merchandise, offering food or animal skins for things they needed, such as sugar or cloth.

how many goods were smuggled or how much money they made from smuggling.

WAR AND PACIFISTS

When war broke out between England and Spain in 1739, Thomas Penn did not want to let the Quakers in the legislature prevent the colony from contributing to defense. He feared he might lose his colony as his father had in 1692. He organized non-Quakers to run for the assembly and hired sailors to bully the voters in the 1742 election. Still, the Quaker candidates won easily. Penn wanted to take away Quaker voting rights, while Quakers planned to ask the Crown to take Pennsylvania over as a royal colony. Ben Franklin, a prominent Philadelphia citizen and a supporter of the Quakers, finally worked out a compromise in the form of a volunteer **militia** in 1748. That way, pacifists could not be forced to fight against their conscience.

So many immigrants of other religions had come to Pennsylvania that by the

Construction began on the Pennsylvania capitol building, called the State House, in 1732. The colonial government first met there in 1741. Later the building would be known as Independence Hall, one of the most famous colonial buildings in America. An English visitor to Philadelphia wrote, "At the upper end of second street is a State House, for the meeting of the Governor and Assembly, but not quite finished when I was there, which when done would be the finest edifice in all America."

1750s Quakers had become a minority group, making up only a quarter of the population. However, many German immigrants supported the Quaker government because it did not tax them to pay for an established church or military forces. The Scotch-Irish, however, who lived on the farthest reaches of the western frontier, wanted the colonial government to support a militia to defend the frontier against Native Americans. They illegally occupied much land belonging to Native Americans, and attacked them at every opportunity. William Penn's sons did nothing to protect the Native Americans, and so finally earned their hatred. When war broke out again, this time between England and France, some of the battles took place in western Pennsylvania. Still, the Quakers in the legislature resisted voting for men and weapons.

Benjamin Franklin

Benjamin Franklin was born in Boston in 1706, one of 17 children. His formal education ended when he was ten years old, but he was hard working and curious, and continued to study and read on his own. Franklin learned the printer's trade from his older brother, but had a bitter disagreement with him. At the age of 17, Ben walked out of his brother's business and moved to Philadelphia, with barely a dollar in his pocket. He went to work for Philadelphia's first newspaper, the American Mercury. By the time Ben Franklin was 24 years old, he owned a major newspaper called the Pennsylvania Gazette. He eventually gained a lasting international reputation for his involvement in writing and publishing, science, public service, and politics.

In 1729 Franklin's printing company received the job of printing paper money for Pennsylvania. He also received printing assignments from the neighboring colonies. In 1732, he began publishing Poor Richard's Almanac, which became very popular. Franklin helped to organize several institutions that were among the first of their kind: a lending library, called the Library Company of Philadelphia, in 1731; Philadelphia's first volunteer firefighting company; the American Philosophical Society in 1743; a nonreligious college called the Academy of Philadelphia, in 1751, which eventually became the University of Pennsylvania; and the Pennsylvania Hospital in 1751. From 1730 to 1774, Franklin was married to Deborah Read, whom he had met when he first arrived in Philadelphia as a young man. They raised two children.

Ben Franklin experimented with electricity, most famously by flying a kite during a lightning storm. He survived his experiment and invented the lightning rod, which protects buildings from direct lightning strikes. Franklin also invented the so-called Franklin stove, which used less air and burned wood more slowly than open fireplaces. The stoves gave out more heat using less wood.

In addition to all his other interests, Ben Franklin entered politics as a clerk to the Pennsylvania colonial assembly in 1736. He later worked as the postmaster for all the northern colonies, and as Pennsylvania's colonial representative to London. He returned from London to serve as a delegate to the Second Continental Congress, and helped draft the Declaration of Independence. In 1776, at the age of 70, Franklin sailed to France to try to obtain French assistance for the Revolution. By so doing, he risked being captured and hanged by the British. The French people Franklin met liked and admired him, a fact that greatly helped the American cause in France.

After the Revolution, Ben Franklin helped negotiate a peace treaty with Great Britain, and later helped create the United States Constitution. When Franklin died at the age of 84, thousands of people attended his funeral.

Poor Richard's Almanac was translated into foreign languages. The French referred to Poor Richard as *Bonhomme Richard*.

5.
BATTLES FOR THE WEST

During the 1740s Pennsylvanians made a treaty with the Iroquois to establish a trading route across the Allegheny mountains into the Ohio River valley. British traders from Pennsylvania and Virginia met with western Native Americans to trade for furs. In exchange the British offered guns and gunpowder, tools, rum, and other merchandise.

Well-known Pennsylvania traders, such as the Irishman George Croghan and the German Conrad Weiser, received warm welcomes from their Native American trading partners. Wrote Weiser in his journal of 1748, "Joy appeared in their countenances ... The Native American Council met this evening to shake hands with me and show their satisfaction at my safe arrival ... I treated them with a quart of whiskey & a roll of tobacco; they expressed their good wishes to King George & all his people & were mighty

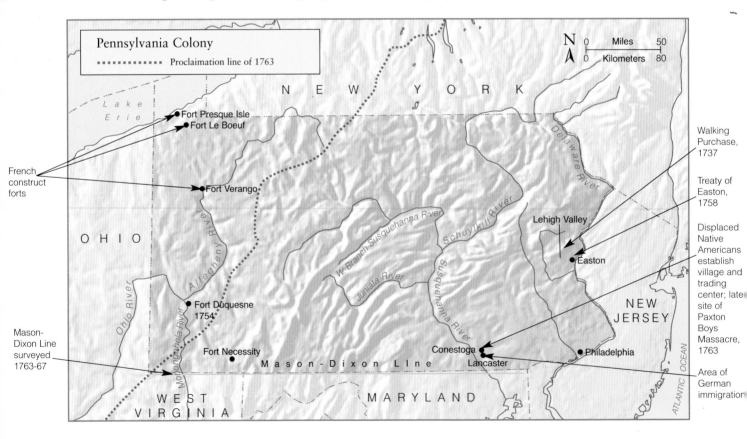

Pennsylvania Colony

- - - - - - Proclaimation line of 1763

N

Miles 0 — 50
Kilometers 0 — 80

Lake Erie

NEW YORK

Fort Presque Isle
Fort Le Boeuf

French construct forts

Fort Verango

OHIO

Allegheny River

Delaware River

Walking Purchase, 1737

Treaty of Easton, 1758

Lehigh Valley

W. Branch Susquehanna River

Schuylkill River

Displaced Native Americans establish village and trading center; later site of Paxton Boys Massacre, 1763

Easton

Juniata River

Susquehanna River

Fort Duquesne 1754

Monongahela River

Mason-Dixon Line surveyed 1763-67

Fort Necessity

Conestoga
Lancaster

Mason-Dixon Line

Philadelphia

NEW JERSEY

ATLANTIC OCEAN

Area of German immigration

WEST VIRGINIA

MARYLAND

This 1755 map shows the colonies reaching straight across the American continent.

pleased that I looked upon them as brethren of the English."

At the same time, French traders were operating from the north and west, entering Indian country from Canada, the Great Lakes, and the Mississippi Valley. The French and British viewed one another as competitors for Native American trade, and they also both wanted to claim the western lands for their countries. British mapmakers of the time drew the colonies' borders in straight lines westward across the continent. Both the French and the British tried to get the Native Americans on their side by giving them gifts. The French traders especially got along well with their Native American trading partners. Many of them lived among the native peoples and married Native American women.

Farmers from the settled parts of Pennsylvania had also moved into the Ohio Valley. Many looked to the Ohio country as the next source of new farmland. However, the British government was paying more attention to wars in Europe than to securing new land in North America.

Neither Pennsylvania nor Virginia were willing to spend money to build forts in the disputed western territory. Then in 1752, Frenchmen led a troop of Native Americans from Canada in an attack on the main British trading post in Ohio country. They massacred and mutilated the outnumbered English and Native Americans at the post. The following year the French built several forts in the western part of modern-day Pennsylvania.

The Virginia governor sent a militia company west in 1754 to build a British fort at the site of present-day Pittsburgh, Pennsylvania. A party of about 500 French and Native American men drove off the outnumbered Virginians, preventing them from completing the fort. Instead, the French completed it and called it Fort Duquesne.

Soon after, the young Virginia colonel, George Washington, arrived with a small force of about 60 men. He was too late to defend the fort. However, Washington heard that some French soldiers were nearby and mounted a surprise attack on them. Washington and his Virginians defeated the small French force. He then ordered the construction of a fort on the site, which he named Fort Necessity. But on July 3, 1754, nearly a thousand French and Native Americans attacked the fort. Washington had no choice but to surrender. This battle marked the beginning of a world war that lasted seven years. In Europe it was called the Seven Years' War, in America, the French and Indian War.

The defeat at Fort Necessity got the attention of the authorities in distant Great Britain. Britain sent a large number of British soldiers to North America to fight the French. In 1755 more than 1,000 troops landed in Virginia under the command of General Edward Braddock. Joined by George Washington and about 450 Virginia and Maryland soldiers, Braddock and his men marched straight across Virginia and into Pennsylvania, intending to retake Fort Duquesne.

As the large army of red-coated British soldiers approached the fort on a narrow wilderness path, they made an easy target for a surprise attack. On July 9, a small force of French and Native American men ambushed the army, shooting from the cover of the woods. In just three hours, they killed or wounded more than 900 of the British soldiers, and lost only 43 of their own. Braddock himself was wounded and died a few days later.

After Braddock's defeat the surviving British regulars marched off to fight in New York, leaving Pennsylvanians to defend their own frontier as best they could. The disastrous defeat had left the western frontier open to numerous and deadly Native American raids. Shawnee and Delawares killed or captured hundreds of settlers and burned their cabins, although they did try to avoid harming Quakers. In 1755 Native Americans massacred

Eighteen-year-old Colonel James Smith of Pennsylvania was working in the western part of the colony in 1755, building a road for the British troops marching to Fort Duquesne. When Smith was ordered to go meet some supply wagons, a group of Delawares ambushed him and took him prisoner. At first he was held at Fort Duquesne, and he saw the French and Indians go out to ambush Braddock and his men. After Braddock's defeat, the Indians brought back prisoners and burned them alive. Smith finally escaped in 1759.

an entire settlement in eastern Pennsylvania's Lehigh Valley. Settlers fled the frontier and retreated back toward Philadelphia.

The Quaker-controlled Pennsylvania assembly still refused to vote money for defense, even when urged by their friend, Benjamin Franklin. They voted instead to investigate the cause of the Native Americans' hostility. Only when protesters dumped scalped and mutilated bodies outside the assembly did the delegates offer a compromise. Once again they allowed people to volunteer for the militia, and voted a sum of money "for the King's use," which they could pretend was not actually for war.

The most important Native American congress in Pennsylvania history took place in Easton. More than 500 Native Americans from thirteen tribal nations met with Pennsylvania officials. There were Delawares from both the eastern and western branches, representatives from all six Iroquois nations, and delegates from many tribes living in the Ohio Valley. The congress concluded with the signing of the Treaty of Easton on October 25 and 26, 1758. The Delawares and the Native Americans from Ohio agreed to stop fighting on the French side. Pennsylvania officials agreed to stop colonists from settling west of the Allegheny Mountains. Peace with the native peoples allowed British and colonial troops to cut a new road through the Pennsylvania wilderness to Fort Duquesne. Abandoned by their Native American allies, the French fled, burning the fort as they left. The British built a new, larger fort and called it Fort Pitt. From then on, white settlers streamed into the area and settled on Native American land, in open defiance of the Treaty of Easton.

The rest of the French and Indian War took place to the north, in New York and in Canada. The British defeated the French at Quebec in 1759 and took control of Canada. In 1763 France and England signed a peace treaty giving the British control of much of North America. Large numbers of new immigrants then began to arrive in the colonies from Great Britain, Germany, and other parts of Europe.

The People of Pennsylvania

Like most colonies, Pennsylvania started with a few hundred European colonists, about 500 in 1681. It grew more rapidly than any other American colony, reaching a population of 8,000 in less than four years. By the time of the Revolution, more than a quarter million colonists lived there. During it's 95-year colonial period, Pennsylvania's population grew so rapidly, more than doubling every 20 years, that it was surpassed only by that of Virginia.

Around the time of the Revolution, 35% of Pennsylvania's white population was English. Another 8% were Scottish, 11% Scotch-Irish, and 3% Irish. Thirty-three percent were German. The German people of Penn-sylvania came to be called, incorrectly, the "Pennsylvania Dutch." The Germans' word for themselves was Deutsch, and English people misunderstood, mispronounced, and misspelled it. Less than 2% of the colony's people were actually Dutch, immigrants from the Netherlands. Another tiny minority were Swedes who had moved from Delaware, a part of Penn's colony that had once been the site of a Swedish colony.

Slavery never caught on in Pennsylvania, a land of family farms worked by the owners, their families, and indentured servants or paid laborers. Most of Pennsylvania's Quakers objected to slavery on moral grounds. In the five years before the Revolution, fewer than three dozen slaves were imported or exported by Pennsylvanians. By 1770 fewer than 6,000 of Pennsylvania's nearly quarter-million people were black.

The western Native Americans protested the arrival of even more British settlers, who occupied their land and drove away the game animals. Many tribes who had never cooperated before worked together to drive the British from their land. Native Americans captured British forts and raided frontier settlements in western Pennsylvania, Virginia, and Maryland. They killed or captured about 2,000 colonists. The British called the attacks "Pontiac's Rebellion," after a western chief.

In revenge for the frontier raids, a gang of Pennsylvania colonists attacked the peaceful remnants of the Native American village, Conestoga. By 1763 only 22 Native Americans remained in Conestoga. In December of that year, a group of 50 men, who called themselves the Paxton Boys, murdered all but two of them. They then marched on Philadelphia to kill Native Americans who had taken refuge there. British troops blocked their way, and the Paxton boys returned home after the authorities promised not to prosecute them for the murders. Many Pennsylvanians were disgusted by the massacre of innocent Native Americans. Ben Franklin called the Paxton Boys "Christian white savages."

When Native Americans threatened to attack Fort Pitt, William Trent, who had once traded with Native Americans, pretended that he still considered them friends. He reported, "Out of our regard for them we gave them two blankets and a handkerchief out of the smallpox hospital. I hope it will have the desired effect." In other words, Trent was resorting to cruel germ warfare.

In order to keep peace with the Native Americans, the British government issued the Proclamation of 1763. This act forbade colonists to settle any land west of the Allegheny Mountains and ordered existing settlers to return east. Settlers and investors who thought they owned land now found that they did not, and they blamed the British government.

6.
CRADLE OF LIBERTY

IMPORT: TO BRING
MERCHANDISE INTO THE
COUNTRY FOR SALE

The French and Indian War had cost Great Britain a lot of money, and the British thought that the colonists should help pay for it. The British Parliament imposed taxes on the colonists, and this enraged them. The first major new tax law was the Sugar Act of 1764. The act called for **import** and export duties, or taxes, to be paid on many trade goods, such as sugar, coffee, indigo, and animal hides. The British sent royal navy ships to patrol the American coast and enforce the law. They also assigned customs officials to collect the taxes and had merchants arrested who were thought to be evading the taxes.

A year later, in 1765, Parliament passed the Stamp Act. Under the Stamp Act, colonists had to pay to have most documents stamped, or risk arrest. Even newspapers had to have stamps. At first, a few Americans thought the Stamp Act was reasonable. Ben Franklin tried to have some of his friends appointed as stamp agents. But the Stamp Act annoyed colonists of all social classes, and

Pennsylvania Hospital, built in
Philadelphia in 1751, was America's
first so-called "general" hospital.

BOYCOTT: AGREEMENT TO REFUSE TO BUY FROM OR SELL TO CERTAIN BUSINESSES OR PEOPLE

BRITISH: NATIONALITY OF A PERSON BORN IN GREAT BRITAIN; PEOPLE BORN IN ENGLAND ARE CALLED "ENGLISH"

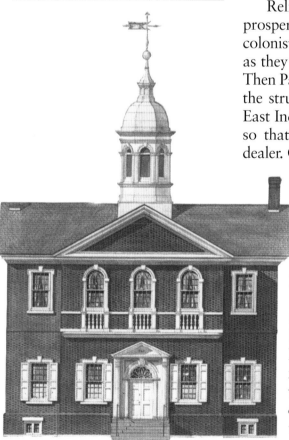

Carpenters' Hall was the borrowed meeting place of the First Continental Congress.

resistance grew throughout the colonies. Riots broke out, and groups calling themselves the Sons of Liberty attacked the offices and homes of tax collectors. So unpopular was the Stamp Act that Parliament repealed it in March 1766. Still, King George III insisted that Great Britain's Parliament had the right to make laws for the colonies and collect taxes. Britain passed a new set of laws taxing even more products, and angering more colonists. Tensions continued to grow between colonists and British soldiers and officials.

The leaders of opposition to British laws formed Committees of Correspondence throughout the colonies. By writing letters, the Committees would keep one another informed and make plans for the colonies to cooperate. They also planned to spread news that would influence public opinion in favor of rebellion. The Committees got all the colonies except New Hampshire to **boycott British** merchandise. The boycott convinced the British to repeal most taxes by 1770, except for the tax on tea.

Relieved of tax burdens for a while, the colonies prospered, and colonial life remained calm until 1773. Few colonists really wanted independence from Britain, as long as they could make their own laws and set their own taxes. Then Parliament passed a law that gave one British tea seller, the struggling East India Company, special treatment. The East India Company was given a monopoly in the colonies, so that it could sell its tea more cheaply than any other dealer. Once again, the Committees of Correspondence went to work, spreading news of the new law and the coming East India Company tea shipments. The Sons of Liberty organized actions against the shipments. The first such action, the famous Boston Tea Party, occurred in December 1773 with the dumping of a large tea shipment into Boston Harbor. Actions in other port cities followed.

Most of Philadelphia's tea merchants sold smuggled tea. In October 1773, 700 people met in Philadelphia and decided to disrupt the sale of East India Company tea. Bullies threatened the merchants who carried the tea, and caused most of them to quit. The *Polly*, a ship carrying tea, was due to arrive in Philadelphia, and the patriots threatened any pilot who might help her into the harbor. The *Polly* arrived at Philadelphia the very day that news of the Boston Tea Party reached the city. A growing mob convinced the ship to head back to its home port.

Britain responded to the Boston Tea Party by passing the Boston Port Act, which closed the port of Boston and placed Massachusetts under military rule. Boston patriot Paul Revere rode all the way to Philadelphia with news of the Boston Port Act, and Philadelphians agreed that they would not try to take over Boston's shipping business. Many in the colonies began to argue that they would have to fight for independence from Great Britain. All the colonies but Georgia agreed to meet in Philadelphia in September 1774.

The First Continental Congress met in Philadelphia's Carpenters' Hall on September 5, 1774. The congress drew up a set of resolutions stating the rights of the colonies to self-government, and formed a Continental Association to boycott British trade goods and organize local governments. Finally, the delegates agreed to meet again in May 1775. Before that date arrived, though, the first battle of the American Revolution had been fought in Massachusetts, on April 19, 1775.

The Second Continental Congress met in May 1775 at Pennsylvania's State House in Philadelphia, the seat of the colony's government. The building was later renamed Independence Hall. At the second congress, the delegates voted to raise a Continental Army, with George Washington as its commander-in-chief. A year later, the congress met at the same place to vote for independence. Benjamin Franklin served on the committee that wrote the Declaration of Independence. Of the 56 men who signed the declaration, issued on July 4, 1776, nine of them were Pennsylvanians.

A few days later, Pennsylvania held a constitutional convention to decide how it would be governed as an independent state. Pennsylvania's new constitution, approved in September 1776, was the first to eliminate property ownership requirements for voting, and allow all adult white male taxpayers to vote.

In Europe, hunting was a special privilege reserved for wealthy landowners and their friends. In America, people prized the right to hunt wild game, such as deer. The right to hunt was made a part of Pennsylvania's first state constitution in 1776. An English visitor remarked in amazement, "Hunting is allowed to them and all others, there being no lords of manors to hamper them with their privileges."

EPILOGUE

The Continental Congress governed the rebelling colonies and conducted the Revolutionary War from Philadelphia, except for the months during which the British threatened or occupied the city. Revolutionary Pennsylvania was the site of several large battles. When the British occupied Philadelphia during the winter of 1777–1778, George Washington took the Continental army into winter quarters at Valley Forge. There the soldiers suffered terribly from cold and hunger, but survived to win their place in history.

Pennsylvania became the second state to ratify the United States Constitution in 1787. Philadelphia served as the nation's capital from 1790 to 1800.

Modern Pennsylvania has a population of about 12 million, 9 percent of whom are African-American. About

Many artists have tried to portray the Continental army's terrible winter at Valley Forge. Two thousand of some 12,000 soldiers died of cold, hunger, and disease.

Reconstructed soldiers' huts at
Valley Forge National Historical Park

11,000 Delaware (Leni-Lenape), Susquehanna, Shawnee, and Iroquois people still live in Pennsylvania.

About half of Pennsylvania is still wooded, but with mostly new growth. Most of the old forests have been cut down, and new trees have grown up in place of the old. Raccoons, foxes, skunks, and deer are still plentiful in some areas. Bears still live in the remote areas, and wildcats have become even more scarce. Pennsylvania's crop and pasture land lies mostly in the southern part of the state. Only about two percent of the population still farms.

Pennsylvania's two largest cities are Philadelphia, still a busy port on the Delaware River, and Pittsburgh in the west, an active port at the head of the Ohio River. About one Pennsylvanian worker in five works in a factory, many producing steel or processing food. Coal mining was once important, but many mines have closed.

The Revolutionary site, Independence Hall, is now part of a national park, as is Valley Forge.

Fort Necessity, where the French and Indian War began, has been reconstructed as a national park. Bethlehem, first settled in 1741, still has a few original **Moravian** buildings, as well as some reconstructed sites.

The Society of Friends, and the Moravian and Mennonite Churches, whose members once took refuge in Pennsylvania, are still active in Pennsylvania and around the world.

Moravian: member of a Christian church formed in Moravia, in eastern Europe, during the 1400s

DATELINE

1643: The capital of New Sweden is built near present-day Philadelphia.

1681: King Charles II grants William Penn land in America and a charter to colonize it. The first colonists of Pennsylvania set sail from England.

1682: William Penn arrives in Pennsylvania and organizes its government. He receives the three counties of Delaware from the Duke of York and adds them to Pennsylvania.

1683: The first German settlers arrive in Pennsylvania.

1684: William Penn returns to England to defend his possession of Delaware from Lord Baltimore.

1692–1694: Pennsylvania is taken over as a royal colony.

1718: William Penn dies in England after a long illness, leaving Pennsylvania to three of his sons.

1737: Thomas Penn swindles the Delaware Native Americans out of a huge piece of land by way of the Walking Purchase.

1754: In western Pennsylvania, the French build Fort Duquesne and Virginians led by George Washington build Fort Necessity. The French force the Virginians to retreat.

1755: The French defeat a large British and colonial force in its attempt to take Fort Duquesne. Known as Braddock's Defeat, the disaster prompts Native Americans to attack frontier settlements.

1758: The British drive the French from Fort Duquesne, and the French destroy the fort as they flee. The British build Fort Pitt in its place. Colonists begin settling the area in spite of a treaty reserving the land for Native Americans.

1763: The Paxton Boys slaughter the defenseless Native Americans living at Conestoga.

1763–1767: Mason and Dixon survey the final border between Pennsylvania and Maryland.

1773: A mob protests the arrival of a tea ship in Philadelphia.

1774: The First Continental Congress meets in Philadelphia.

1775: The Second Continental Congress meets in Philadelphia.

1776: Congress votes for independence from Great Britain and the Declaration of Independence is signed in Philadelphia. Pennsylvania approves a state constitution.

1777–78: The rebel and British armies battlearound Philadelphia

1787: Pennsylvania becomes the second state to ratify the U.S. Constitution.

Glossary

ALLIANCE: agreement to cooperate, or to fight on the same side in a war

AMERICA: land that contains the continents of North America and South America

AMISH: member of a religious group, founded by Jacob Amman, that split from the Mennonites

APPRENTICE: person who learns a craft or trade by working for a master

BOYCOTT: agreement to refuse to buy from or sell to certain businesses or people

BRITISH: nationality of a person born in Great Britain; people born in England are called "English"

CHARTER: document containing the rules for running an organization

COLONY: land owned and controlled by a distant nation; a colonist is a permanent settler of a colony.

CROWN: KING OR QUEEN OF ENGLAND

CURRENCY: coins or paper used as money

DRAFT HORSE: type of large horse specially bred to pull heavy loads

EPIDEMIC: widespread outbreak of contagious disease; for example, in 1639, a smallpox epidemic killed half of all Huron Native Americans

EXPORT: to send merchandise out of the country for sale

FRONTIER: newest place of settlement, located the farthest away from the center of population

GRANT: formal gift of a parcel of land

GREAT BRITAIN: nation formed by England, Wales, Scotland, and Northern Ireland; "Great Britain" came into use when England and Scotland formally unified in 1707

IMMIGRANT: person who enters a new country to settle there permanently

IMPORT: to bring merchandise into the country for sale

INDIANS: name given to all Native Americans at the time Europeans first came to America, because it was believed that America was actually a close neighbor of India

IROQUOIS CONFEDERACY: the alliance formed by the Mohawk, Onondaga, Oneida, Seneca, and Cayuga N.A. around 1570, and later joined by the Tuscaroras from North Carolina

LEGISLATURE: group of representatives elected to make laws

MENNONITE: member of a Christian church formed in Switzerland in 1525

MERCHANT: trader; person who buys and re-sells merchandise

MILITIA: group of citizens not normally part of the army who join together to defend their land in an emergency

MORAVIAN: member of a Christian church formed in Moravia, in eastern Europe, during the 1400s

PACIFIST: person against war and violence; the beliefs of such a person

PARLIAMENT: legislature of Great Britain

PENNSYLVANIA DUTCH: the popular name incorrectly applied to Germans living in Pennsylvania

PERSECUTE: punish people because of their beliefs, religion, or race

PIG IRON: product created by smelting iron ore in a furnace

PROPRIETOR: private owner

QUAKER: originally a term of mockery given to members of the Society of Friends, a Christian group founded in England around 1650

SCOTCH-IRISH: Scottish people who settled in northern Ireland during the early 1600s. Many were driven by poverty to emigrate to America as indentured servants

SMALLPOX: highly contagious and widespread disease that caused painful skin eruptions, scarring, and often death, until it was nearly wiped out by vaccination in the 20th century. The disease did not occur among Native Americans in America until they caught it from the first Europeans. Having no resistance to the new disease, huge numbers of Native Americans died.

SMUGGLER: one who secretly and illegally trades in forbidden merchandise, or who conceals the merchandise to avoid paying taxes on it

SURPLUS: extra

FURTHER READING

Collier, Christopher, and James Lincoln Collier. *The French and Indian War, 1660–1763.* Tarrytown, N.Y.: Marshall Cavendish, 1998.

Doherty, Kieran. *William Penn, Quaker Colonist.* Brookfield, Conn.: Millbrook Press, 1998.

Franklin, Benjamin. *Autobiography & Other Writings.* New York: Oxford University Press, 1999.

Russell, Francis. *The French and Indian Wars.* New York: American Heritage Publishing Co., 1962.

Smith, Carter, ed. *Battles in a New Land: A Source Book on Colonial America.* Brookfield, CT: Millbrook Press, 1991.

Smith, Carter, ed. *Daily Life: A Source Book on Colonial America.* Brookfield, Conn.: Millbrook Press, 1991.

WEBSITES

www.americaslibrary.gov
Select "Jump back in time" for links to history activities.

http://www.fortedwards.org/cwffa/cwffhome.htm
Explore frontier forts involved in the French and Indian War.
www.nps.gov/fone/relsites.htm

Disclaimer

BIBLIOGRAPHY

Harpster, John W., ed. *Pen Pictures of Early Western Pennsylvania.* Pittsburgh: University of Pittsburgh Press, 1938.

Illick, Joseph E. *Colonial Pennsylvania: A History.* New York: Charles Scribner's Sons, 1976.

Middleton, Richard. *Colonial America: A History, 1607–1760.* Cambridge, Mass: Blackwell, 1992.

Myers, Albert Cook. *Narratives of Early Pennsylvania, West New Jersey, and Delaware: 1630–1707.* New York: Charles Scribner's Sons, 1912.

Taylor, Alan. *American Colonies.* New York: Viking, 2001.

The American Heritage History of the Thirteen Colonies. New York: American Heritage, 1967.

INDEX

JUV
974.802
Wiener   Wiener, Roberta

          Pennsylvania